Serial Killers True Crime:

13 Serial Killer Murder Stories of the 90s

Daniel Brand

TABLE OF CONTENTS

Introduction

Congratulations on purchasing *Serial Killers True Crime: 13 Serial Killer Murder Stories of the 90s* and thank you for doing so. The 1990s was a time of great technological and social change in America, but it was also a time when monsters stalked the highways and byways of the country as well as, for the first time, the information super highway.

The following chapters will discuss in detail the life and times of Herbert Richard Baumeister, Rory Enrique Conde, Harvey Miguel Robinson, Charles Edmund Cullen, Jeffery Lionel Dahmer, Gary Charles Evan, Scott William Cox, Keith Hunter Jesperson ,Orville Lynn Majors, Cleophus Price Jr, David Parker Ray, John

Edward Robinson and Michael Swango. These men all, for one reason or another, decided to cross the line between man and monster and take the lives of innocent people in cold blood. Inside you will learn about their childhoods and lives before the murders began, the periods in their lives that made them famous, how they were eventually arrested and more.

There are plenty of books on this subject on the market, thanks again for choosing this one! Every effort was made to ensure it is full of as much useful information as possible, please enjoy!

Chapter 1
HERBERT RICHARD BAUMEISTER

Born: April 7, 1947

Died: July 3, 1996

AKA: Brian Smart

Active in: Westfield Indiana

Sentenced to: N/A (Suicide)

Herbert Baumeister allegedly killed at least 20 men during the late 80s up until the mid-90s in Indiana. He would pick up men of a similar description at gay bars, murder them and then dispose of the bodies either on his property, Fox Hollow Farms, or along isolated stretches of the I-70. When he learned that his property had been searched in 1996, Baumeister fled to Canada and killed himself.

Early Life

Herbert Richard Baumeister was the oldest of Herbert and Elizabeth Baumeister's four children. While nothing known in his early childhood history could be said to directly influence his later actions, classmates would later recall that he was often seen playing with dead animals and on one occasion even brought a dead bird to class and left it on his teacher's desk. As he grew older, he started to exhibit a wide range of antisocial behaviors including urinating on his teachers' desks on more than one occasion. He was diagnosed with schizophrenia as a teen but never received any recorded treatment for the condition.

He spent a semester at Indiana University in 1965 and then again in 1967 as well as a semester at Butler in 1972. As a young adult he held numerous different jobs at which he would prove competent before ultimately before leaving or being fired after some type of bizarre behavior disrupted the workplace. While these issues never resulted in any legal complaints, they continued to showcase the types of antisocial and schizophrenic behavior he had displayed in his younger years.

By 1971 Baumeister was seeing Juliana Saiter whom he would marry later that year. Only a few months into their marriage, Baumeister was committed to a mental institution by his father where he stayed for two months. Between 1979 and 1981 he and Juliana would go on to have three children. In 1974 he started working for the Bureau of Motor Vehicles and by 1985 had worked his way up to Program Director. He ultimately lost his job when he urinated on a letter that was then sent to the governor of Indiana. This was the same year that the body of Eric Roetiger, a young white male, and Baumeister's theoretical first victim, was found.

In 1988, Baumeister received a loan from his mother and started the SAV-A-LOT thrift store, which quickly became a success. The business expanded to a second location almost immediately and by 1991 was so successful that the Baumeister family was able to move to the luxurious Fox Hollow Farm which Herb's activities would eventually make famous. The move represented a change in status for the family and Herb was now viewed as a pillar of the community.

Murders

During this time, it is believed that Baumeister started frequenting gay bars in the area. He would seek out victims that met his specifications and then lure them back to his pool house by posing as someone who was interested in autoerotic asphyxiation and then invite his victims to participate with him. Once the men were intoxicated and on his property, or presumably in his vehicle, he would then strangle them to death. His murder spree continued throughout Indiana and Ohio and by 1992 police in the Indianapolis area started noticing that a fair number of gay men of similar appearance, weight, height and age seemed to be disappearing.

Investigators were eventually contacted by a man who claimed to have escaped from someone using the name Brian Smart who had killed another man using a pool hose and who had also attempted to do the same to him. Detectives then started canvasing gay bars in the area and eventually were able to track the license plate of the car of someone matching Brian Smart's description to Herb Baumeister.

Officers in the investigation asked to search Fox Hollow Farm and were initially rebuffed by both Baumeister and his wife. As they didn't have anything concrete on Baumeister other than he matched the description of Smart, and due to the fact that the murder of gay men didn't seem to warrant much public interest at the time, the investigation ended up on hold. It was reopened four years later when Juliana Baumeister filed for divorce from her husband after his mood swings reached epic proportions. Freed from her previous marital obligations, she now granted the police access to the property.

In the interim, things took a downturn for Baumeister who had started to come to work reeking of booze as he watched his once flourishing business fail. In 1994, the eldest Baumeister child Erich, found a human skull on the family's property and brought it to his mother. Juliana asked her husband about it and was told that it had come from a medical skeleton that had once belonged to his father. When Juliana later went looking for these remains they could not be found.

With the proper permission granted, the search of Fox Hollow Farm was conducted while

Baumeister was out of town on vacation. The investigation crew hit pay dirt almost immediately. All told they found the remains of eleven men, three of whom are yet to be identified. Eventually, nine additional suspects who met the general description of the bodies found on the property were found buried throughout rural regions of Interstate 70.

Capture

Learning of the discovery on his property while he was on vacation, Baumeister fled to Canada where he ultimately committed suicide in Pinery Provincial park by shooting himself in the head. His suicide note referenced his failing business and marriage, no mention of his flight to Canada or the murders was listed.

Chapter 2
RORY ENRIQUE CONDE

Born: June 14, 1965
Died: N/A
AKA: The Tamiami Trail Strangler
Active in: Miami Florida
Sentenced to: Death

Rory Enrique Conde, aka the Tamiami Trail Strangler killed six prostitutes over a five-month span in 1994-95. He strangled his victims before sodomizing their dead bodies and dumping them along the trail which lent him its name. He is currently awaiting the death penalty along with serving five consecutive life sentences for the murders.

Early life

Rory Conde was born and raised in Barranquilla Colombia. When he was young, his mother died from tetanus and he and his sister went to live with their paternal grandparents. This lasted for about six years and when he was twelve they went to live with his father in Miami. Conde never liked his father and has said on several occasions that he was emotionally abusive. Conde's wife would later indicate that she believed he had been sexually abused as a child as well.

When Conde was twenty-one, he married Carla Conde who was fifteen. They had two children together and Conde proved to be an abusive father and husband and a span of jail time in 1992 resulted from a fight between Rory and Carla over his bringing other women back to their home. This was not an isolated incident as Conde had always had a penchant for prostitutes, but this latest episode was way beyond what had come before.

By 1994, the couple's marriage was crumbling and Conde's habits had not changed. At one point, he brought home a prostitute, dressed her in his wife's lingerie and filmed their time together. This was the last straw for Carla, who found out about the tape and promptly took the children and moved in with her parents, leaving Rory in their Tamiami Trail condo all along. She later reported that Rory had threatened to kill her if she started dating anyone else.

Murders

Conde's murderous escapades began on September 17, 1994 when he killed a transvestite prostitute named Lazaro Comensana. When he is eventually questioned about the murder, Conde maintains that he killed the man after finding out he wasn't actually a woman in the midst of oral sex. He admits that he was angry about the deception but also angry about what had happened to his marriage, and that he blamed prostitutes, not himself, as the cause of his current predicament.

The first murder occurred in the heat of the moment, after the deed was done Conde made the sign of the cross over the body, redressed it and then put it in his car. He dumped the body in a middle-class neighborhood, where it was promptly found the next morning. Instead of making him feel better however, the first murder just stirred up something in Conde and he soon killed an additional pair of prostitutes. On October 8, 1994 he killed Elisa Martinez and then he killed Charity Nava a few weeks later on November 20. Each body was dumped in the same way after the fact.

With Nava, he also left a note for the police on her back and buttocks. He wrote the word third with an exclamation point, taking care to use a smiley face to dot the exclamation point. He also indicated that he would be contacting local news personality WPLG anchor Dwight Lauderdale. Finally, he taunted law enforcement to see if they could catch him using a pair of eyes as a stand in for see.

While he never actually reached out to the anchor, the local media was abuzz with stories related to the Tamiami Trail Strangler. The victims even each received tragic news pieces that minimized their troubled pasts and focused on the horrible crimes that had been committed against them.

From there, Conde went on to kill three more prostitutes in the span of three months. He killed Wanda Crawford just days after Charity Nava on November 25; Necole Schneider almost a month later on December 17 and then finally Rhonda Dunn on January 12. While his previous victims had all been chosen based on their general convenience, after the fact it was clear that Dunn had been chosen because she bore a striking resemblance to Conde's wife. Each of his victims was strangled to death and then sodomized after the act was completed.

Capture

Conde was apprehended in June 1995 when Gloria Maestre, who was to be his next victim, made enough noise from where she was bound to attract the attention of his neighbors. At the time, Conde was out of his home and in court to plea to a shoplifting charge. When the police burst in they found Maestre who admitted that she had willingly accompanied Conde in the home in order to engage in sexual activity. However, once inside, he had bound and then raped her repeatedly before binding her more tightly and going to the courthouse.

While in the home, one of the officers noticed a green beeper of the same type that was known to have been stolen from another dead prostitute from a few months before. That prostitute, Charity Nava, had already been linked via DNA evidence at the crime scene to the other five murders that Conde had committed. Based on this evidence, and the testimony of the latest victim, the police were able to take Conde into custody where he soon confessed to the crimes.

He was ultimately sentenced to death in 2000 for the murder of Rhonda Dunn before then pleading guilty to the murder of his other victims as well. He is currently serving five consecutive life terms without the possibility of parole while he tries to appeal his death sentence conviction.

Chapter 3
HARVEY MIGUEL ROBINSON

Born: December 6, 1974

Died: N/A

AKA: N/A

Active in: Allentown, Pennsylvania

Sentenced to: Death (stayed)/life in prison with additional charges pending

Harvey Miguel Robinson has the dubious honor of being one of the youngest serial killers in American history, being just 18 when he was arrested for the crimes he had committed. Robinson killed two women and a teenager, in addition to trying to kill a child and the woman that would ultimately lead to his capture. Robinson's murder spree was the inspiration for the movie *No One Could Protect Her* starring Joanna Kerns as intended victim Denise Sam-Cali.

Early life

Born in Allentown Pennsylvania, Robinson is the only serial killer ever from the area. His father was a raging alcoholic who routinely abused his mother, both emotionally and physically. By the time Robinson was 3, his parents were divorced and his father eventually left the family and ended up in prison for beating his girlfriend to death so severely that the body was practically unrecognizable. Despite these serious issues, Robinson always admired his father, likely why he was so anxious to begin following in his footsteps.

As a child, Robinson showed an early prowess for sports along with substantial academic potential. This potential was quickly overshadowed by negative behavior, however and he was frequently admonished for stealing women's underwear and was arrested for the first time at just 9 years old. In school, his teachers quickly began noting that he seemed to have a hard time telling right from wrong coupled with an extreme dislike of authority figures of all types. As he grew older, threats and emotional and physical outbursts became common and everyone in the school, students and teachers alike, started to watch their step around the budding serial killer. Between the ages of 9 and 17 he filled up his rap sheet with a wide variety of crimes including resisting arrest and petty burglary.

Murders

Robinson's first victim, Joan Burghardt, was a 29-year-old nurse's aide in August of 1992. He had already visited her home once, and stolen $50 from her bedroom dresser a few days earlier, but he wasn't quite done with her. He returned to the scene of the crime, broke through the screen in the window while she was changing, raped and murdered her in short order and escaped the scene without incident.

Three days later, Burghardt's neighbors called the police to tell them she had left her stereo on for three days straight and the body was promptly discovered having been badly beaten as Robinson felt the need to follow in his father's footsteps. An autopsy showed that she had been hit nearly 40 times, causing severe damage to the skull and brain. Police began a manhunt for the murderer, completely unaware that Robinson had already been picked up on unrelated burglary charges for which he would go on to serve 8 months in prison while the murder of Burghardt would go on to become a cold case for which there were no leads.

Released from prison with the previous year's murder a distant memory, Robinson was then free to target Charlotte Schmoyer a 15-year newspaper carrier on June 9, 1993 whom he raped and then stabbed more than 20 times before slashing her throat. Local residents woke to find their newspapers not in their accustomed places, and one found her paper cart and abandoned bicycle. Her radio headset was found soon after, and then a search party located blood, a shoe and ultimately Schmoyer's body hidden under a stack of logs. After murdering Schmoyer and dumping the body, Robinson was pulled over for speeding and was nearly arrested, he managed to get away with a citation, however, though it would be his final victim who would pay for it.

This victim was Jessica Jean Fortney a 47-year-old grandmother whom Robinson targeted in July 1993. His method of attack was the same, he broke into her home, raped and murdered her, this time via strangulation. His next victim was to be a 5-year-old girl whom he stalked for several days before repeating the process of rape and strangulation, though the little girl was lucky enough to walk away with her life, though not from lack of trying on Robinson's part.

Capture

Robinson's final intended victim was Denise Sam-Cali, as she managed to survive the experience. His methods were much the same for Sam-Cali whom he followed for several days in order to her learn her patterns and habits. When he saw his opportunity, he broke into her home, raped her and then choked her until he believed she was dead. She managed to escape from her home, and even fended off Robinson when he attacked again in order to lose him in the resulting pursuit.

Making her way to the police, Sam-Cali explained her story and then agreed to allow herself to be used as bait to capture Robinson. She returned to her home under police surveillance in order to wait for Robinson to attempt to finish the job. The plan worked and Robinson was injured in the resulting shootout with the police when he broke in. He managed to flee the scene by smashing through a glass window but was then arrested when he went to the hospital for treatment of his wounds.

Despite the fact that juvenile offenders are typically offered some level of leniency for their crimes, the local outcry around the case, coupled with the speed of his crimes and their grisly nature, Robinson was sentenced to death for his crimes initially. However, his execution was officially stayed in 2006. He then went back to trial where he was sentenced to life in prison for murdering Joan Burghardt as the murder occurred when he was a minor. In 2010 he went before another jury for the murder of Charlotte Schmoyer where he exchanged his right to an appeal for a life sentence. He was sentenced to death for the murder of Jessica Fotney, and that conviction is currently being appealed.

Chapter 4
CHARLES EDMUND CULLEN

Born: February 22, 1960

Died: N/A

AKA: N/A

Active in: New Jersey, Pennsylvania

Sentenced to: 127 years in prison

C harles Edmund Cullen is a former nurse and the most prolific serial killer in the history of the East Coast, if not in all of American. He has confessed to killing more than 40 people during his time as a nurse, and subsequent interviews have indicated that the actual number could be far, far, greater as he cannot remember names but can remember specifics of the events. All told, experts believe he may have killed as many as 400 people.

Early life

Cullen was the youngest of 8 children and his father died when he was less than a year old. He has since described his childhood as absolutely miserable and first attempted suicide at the age of 9 when he drank all of the chemicals in a chemistry set he received as a birthday present. This would be the first of many suicide attempts throughout his life.

When he was 17 his mother died and he dropped out of high school in order to join the Navy. There he quickly rose through the ranks until he achieved the rank of petty officer third class working on a submarine and was placed directly in charge of its missile systems. At this point he began showing signs of chronic mental instability as was transferred to a less stressful position on a supply ship instead. While he was in the Navy, Cullen tried to kill himself as many as 7 times before being discharged in 1984.

That very same year he enrolled in nursing school in Montclair New Jersey where he would go on to be elected as the president of his nursing class. He graduated from the program without incident and took a nursing job at the St. Barnabas Medical Center in Livingston New Jersey.

Murders

The first murder that Cullen confessed to took place in June of 1988 while he was working at St. Barnabas. He administered a lethal overdose of medication to Judge John W. Yengo who was in the hospital after suffering a negative reaction to some blood thinning medication. The death was ruled an accident and Cullen was not penalized and allowed to continue interacting with patients. With his first murder proceeding so smoothly, Cullen then stepped up his activities and killed many other patients including an AIDS patient whom he killed with an overdose of insulin.

Cullen left St. Barabas in early 1992 after authorities in the hospital began correctly closing in on him for contaminating a number of IV bags that had gone on to kill more than a dozen patients in the hospital. He moved on to Warren Hospital in Phillipsburg, New Jersey. There he murdered a number of elderly women by overdosing them on a type of heart medication known as digoxin. One of the victims survived and even complained about a sneaky male nurse coming into her room at night to inject her with things but hospital staff and her family members dismissed this paranoia.

In March of 1993, Cullen broke into the home of a coworker while she and her son slept, then left without waking them. This started a new pattern of behavior for Cullen who began stalking the woman to the point that she took out a restraining order against him. He pled guilty to one count of trespassing for which he received a year's probation. This sent Cullen into a period of depression and he took a leave of absence from work and attempted suicide several more times.

In 1994, he began working for Hunterdon Medical Center in Flemington, New Jersey. He doesn't claim to have killed anyone during his first few years there but the records from the period of time he worked at the hospital had been destroyed by the time he was arrested for his crimes. He has admitting to murdering at least 5 patients throughout 1996, once again using overdoses of digoxin to do the deed.

In February 1998, Cullen started work at the Liberty Nursing and Rehabilitation Center in Allentown Pennsylvania where he worked with patients who required respirators. He was fired after being accused of giving patients incorrect drugs and dosages of drugs and was seen entering the room of a patient with syringes in hand right before that patient died, though the death was attributed to another nurse.

From there he worked at Easton Hospital in Easton, Pennsylvania where he killed more patients in the fall of 1998 and the spring of 1999 using digoxin. Despite his mental instability and history of shoddy conduct, the national nursing shortage at the time help to ensure Cullen remained employed. He next worked at the burn unit of the Lehigh Valley Hospital in Allentown where he murder another patient and attempted to murder several more.

Next he moved on to St. Luke's Hospital where he killed at least 5 patients and attempted to kill several more. In early 2000, a coworker noticed vials of mundane drugs in a disposal bin. As the drugs did not have a street value, the theft seemed curious. The theft was linked back to Cullen and the hospital agreed to let him go with a neutral recommendation. At the same time, some of his coworkers got together to tell the local district attorney that they believed he was killing patients. The case was dropped after 9 months due to lack of evidence.

Capture

Finally, Cullen began working at Somerset Medical Center where the changing times finally caught up to him. The hospital used a computerized system for dispensing medication and Cullen was seen misusing the system time and again. Later that year, the New Jersey Poison Information and Education System contacted the hospital to let them know that four suspicious overdoses had been seen from the hospital that year which meant an employee could be killing patients. The hospital didn't do anything with the information for another 3 months, during which time Cullen killed 5 more patients.

When a patient died of low blood sugar in October 2003, the hospital alerted authorities and an investigation into Cullen's history soon followed. Cullen was fired and it was another nurse, Amy Loughren who alerted police to what he had been doing. Cullen was then arrested in December of 2003 and charged with a single count of murder and one count of attempted murder. After his arrest, Cullen admitted that he had killed at least 40 people. In April 2004, he plead guilty to the killing of 13 patients via lethal injection as was sentenced to over 100 years in prison without the possibility of parole.

Chapter 5
JEFFREY LIONEL DAHMER

Born: May 21, 1960

Died: November 28, 1994 (murdered)

AKA: Milwaukee Cannibal

Active in: Milwaukee Wisconsin

Sentenced to: 16 life terms

Perhaps the most well-known serial killer of the decade, Jeffrey Lionel Dahmer, more often known as the Milwaukee-based serial killer who was known to favor cannibalism as well as necrophilia in addition to the confirmed murder and dismemberment of 17 boys and men throughout the 70s, 80s and 90s. As time passed he also started collecting preserved body parts and even entire skeletal structures. Despite being diagnosed with several mental disorders, he was declared sane enough to stand trial where he was convicted of 15 of the 16 murders he committed in Wisconsin and later for an additional murder he committed in Ohio. He received a total of 16 life sentences but was beaten to death by another inmate in November of 1994.

Early life

Dahmer was the eldest of two sons born to Lionel and Joyce Dahmer. He was generally thought to be doted on by both parents as an infant and toddler, though his mother was known to be argumentative with both the neighbors and her husband on a regular basis. When Dahmer was 7 years old, his mother started spending a large amount of time in bed recovering from illnesses both real and imagined and his father was absorbed with his studies at Marquette University and when he was home his attention was focused on his ailing wife. As time went on, Joyce's conditioned worsened to the point where she would work herself into a frenzy over the most trivial of matters, just to watch her husband try and pacify her. She even once went so far as to attempt suicide.

While his father's attention was focused on his mother, Dahmer became withdrawn. He remembers his early years as being full of tension between his parents who were constantly at one another's throats. In school he was seen as both timid and quiet by his peers and his first-grade teacher noted in his report card that she believed that he felt neglected at home. Despite his demeanor, he was known to keep a small group of friends.

Dahmer had always been interested in animals, starting at a very young age, and his interest first manifested in collecting a number of large insects which he kept in jars. This interest eventually started manifesting itself in more gruesome ways as he began to find the carcasses of dead animals and then dismember them before storing various parts in jars in his family's toolshed. One particularly gruesome display was seen by a friend who found the head of a dog impaled on a spike behind Dahmer's house.

Dahmer had always been interested in dead animals, it seems, as his father recalled an instance when his son was no more than 4 and he was removing the bones of an animal that had died beneath the family's home. He recalled how his son seemed especially fascinated with the sound the bones made when then clinked together so much so, in fact, that he started looking for animal bones to play with and started poking the bodies of living animals to determine where their bones were located.

When he reached puberty, Dahmer discovered he was a homosexual, a fact that he kept from his family. Thoughts of dominance and control over a subservient partner often dominated his sexual fantasies and slowly but surely this idea worked its way into his dissection habit as well. His first planned act of violence was to be on a local jogger he saw in the area near his home on a regular basis. He planned to knock the man unconscious and use his body for sexual acts before he awakened. On the day the attack was to take place the man did not appear and he did not try again.

Murders

Dahmer's first murder occurred in 1978, just a few weeks after he had graduated from highs school. He was living alone in his family's home as his parents had gotten a divorce and his mother took his brother to live with family while his father was staying temporarily in a motel in order to be closer to his work. The murder occurred on June 18, when Dahmer picked up a hitchhiker by the name of Steven Mark Hicks and took him back to his house to have a drink.

According to Dahmer, several hours later Hicks wanted to leave which Dahmer then tried to prevent. He struck Hicks twice in the back of the head using a 10-pound dumbbell. When this rendered Hicks unconscious, Dahmer then strangled him, stripped him unconscious and masturbated over the body. Still not satisfied, however, he then took the corpse to the home's crawlspace and dissected the body before burying it in a shallow grave in his backyard. A few weeks later he exhumed the body, removed the flesh from the bones, dissolved it in acid and the smashed the bones using a sledgehammer and scattered the dust.

Dahmer spent the next several years drinking heavily and failing to hold down a job, including a stint in the army where he reportedly raped at least two fellow soldiers. By 1985 he was living in West Allis with his grandmother, the only family member he was said to have liked. He was working nights at the Milwaukee Ambrosia Chocolate Factory when that January, a man propositioned him while at the library. While he didn't act on the invitation, this note reawakened old desires in Dahmer and he began to familiarize himself with Milwaukee's gay scene. He began spending time at local bathhouses, only to find that he did not receive satisfaction when his partners moved around.

This led to the use of sleeping pills in his sexual activity and he regularly gave them to his victims before raping their unconscious bodies. This proved not to be enough for Dahmer, however and he started killing again in November of 1987. It was then he picked up a man named Steven Tuomi and took him to the Ambassador hotel. Dahmer apparently blacked out as he awoke the next morning with Tuomi's body beaten to death underneath him and no memory of having done the deed. Nevertheless, he disposed of the body and did not go to the police. He did, however, keep Tuomi's skull as a memento of the event.

After Tuomi's murder, Dahmer started to seek new victims more regularly, and each of which he would lure to his grandmother's house, drug, rape and kill. This continued until September of 1988 when his grandmother asked him to move out because of his late-night activities and the odd smells coming from the garage as well as the basement. He was soon after arrested for drugging and fondling a 13-year-old boy, however, and moved back into her home.

The first victim of whom Dahmer kept a body part was named Anthony Sears who Dahmer murdered in March of 1989. He ultimately dismembered the body but preserved the head and genitals in acetone before storing them in his locker at work because he "found Sears exceptionally attractive." Dahmer's killings grow more gruesome from there, and he began taking pictures of the bodies in various suggestive positions and preserving and painting the skulls of each of his victims. The first victim that he began experimenting with cannibalism on was named Ernest Miller, he was killed with a knife after Dahmer ran out of sleeping pills and couldn't drug him into unconsciousness.

Capture

In July of 1991, Dahmer reached out to a group of men with an offer to come back to his apartment to pose for nude photographs in exchange for $100. Of the trio, Tracy Edwards agreed and when they reached Dahmer's apartment he was handcuffed and threatened with a knife. He was ultimately able to punch Dahmer in the face and knock him off balance enough to run out the front door. He quickly flagged down a pair of passing policemen and asked that they remove the handcuffs. When their keys didn't fit, he agreed to go with them back to Dahmer's apartment.

Dahmer let the officers into his home and told them that the handcuff key was in the bedroom. Once in the room, the officer noticed an open drawer which contained a large number of polaroid pictures of bodies in various states of decay and were clearly taken in the room in which he was standing. When Dahmer saw what the officer was holding, he attempted to escape but was quickly overpowered. When it was clear he was not going to win, Dahmer reportedly uttered, "For what I did I should be dead."

An investigation of the apartment ended up revealing 4 severed heads, 7 skulls, collected blood drippings, a piece of arm muscles and two human hearts in the refrigerator, an entire torso and a bag of assorted organs in the freezer, two complete skeletons, a pair of severed hands, a mummified scalp, two penises and three more torsos dissolving in acid in a barrel in the bedroom. Dahmer confessed to his crimes almost at once.

Chapter 6
GARY CHARLES EVANS

Born: October 7, 1954
Died: November 14, 1998
AKA: Louis Murray
Active in: New York, Florida, Massachusetts
Sentenced to: N/A (suicide prior to trial)

Unlike many of the people in these pages, Gary Charles Evans didn't kill for perverse mental reasons or to fill some hole that was empty inside of himself, he did it because it was easier to steal from the dead than the living. Whether that makes him less of a monster, or more, is up to you. All told, he admitted to killing 5 people over a 10-year span that ran the length of the east coast.

Early life

As a young child in Troy, New York, Evans routinely suffered beatings at the hands of both Roy and Flor Mae Lee Evans. His mother was mentally unstable and attempted suicide on multiple occasions, once actually shooting her husband in the shoulder when a weapon misfired. Later in life Evans claimed that his father raped him when he was 8 years old. His parents divorced when he was 14 and remarried and divorced again three more times before declaring she was a lesbian 3 years later.

Evans began stealing at a young age, and at the age of 8 brought home a ring that was worth more than $1,000. He emulated his mother, who was also a thief, and also regularly stole things like candy and comic books. By the age of 15 he has graduated to petit larceny for which he receives 90 days in jail. At the age of 22 he is once again caught in the act of robbing a home and is given 4 years in prison, of which he does 2. Once out of prison he goes right back to committing burglaries and is soon caught with a few hundred dollars of stolen goods, enough to send him back to prison.

While in the county jail awaiting his transfer to prison, Evans escapes with the help of a pair of Hells Angels, though he is soon apprehended. He ends up going to spend the rest of his time in prison at Attica State Prison and it was here he first started to consider murder as a viable option. His history of violence and time in prison continues unabated for the rest of his life.

Murders

Evans commits his first murder in July of 1985, using a .22 caliber pistol with a homemade silencer to kill Michael Falco in the midst of an argument about the take from a recent job. He and his primary accomplice Tim Rysedorph wrap the body in a sleeping bag and put it into the trunk of Tim's car. The argument had been about a necklace that Rysedorph had given to a woman but claimed Falco had stolen.

Ending up back in prison, though not for the murder, Evans befriends famous serial killer David Berkowitz, the Son of Sam Killer. Back on the streets in September of 1989, Evans shot Douglas Berry who was sleeping in his store after hours when Evans came in to rob the place. Evans left a shell from the murder on the ground and did not have time to move the body so it was soon found.

Only a few months later in January, Evans killed Damien Cuomo by shooting him 3 times in the head after handcuffing his hands behind his back. He wrapped the body in a shower curtain and buried it in a shallow hole he had already dug for this purpose. He placed a wooden board across the top of the hole and covered it in brush and topsoil and the body was not found until Evans revealed it sometime later. The murder occurred over a disagreement on a job when Evans believed that Cuomo had stiffed him.

In late 1991, Evans spent two weeks casing a jewelry and coin shop from the roof of a nearby building. When the time was right, he walked into the shop and asked the owner, Gregory Jouben to show him a piece of merchandise inside a locked cabinet so he could see what key was used and then shot the man twice in the chest, rolled the body in a rug, placed the rug in his vehicle and then later dismembered and buried it. The community was outraged at one of the few murders that happened in the area each year but Evans was already gone by the time the body was found and nothing was located at the scene to point anyone in his direction.

In 1993, Evans used much the same tactic to steal over 800 antiques from a group antique shop in Vermont after shooting the proprietor that was on site. Later that year he attempted to use a stolen engine crane to steal a bench that weighed more than 1,000 pounds from a cemetery in Albany. He then ended up in jail after his fence became nervous at the last minute and turned him in.

The next year, Evans decided to help the authorities uncover information on another murderer Jeffrey Williams who they believed committed a high-profile murder in the area. After Williams was found guilty of the single murder, Evans walked free despite being guilty for at least 4 murders by this point himself.

His final murder took place in 1997 and was his former accomplice Tim Rysedorph. Once again, the issue was over the take on a particular job. He shot Rysedorph 3 times in the back of the head and then used a chainsaw to dismember the body before transporting it to Brunswick,

New York where he tossed it into a ditch near the interstate.

Capture

Evans was arrested once again in 1998. Once in custody he was apparently tired of running as he confessed to all five murders, before leading police to where the bodies were buried. He tried to escape from the van while being transported to prison by using a shackle key he had secreted in his nose. Free of his restraints, he kicked out the window before jumping from the prison van. On the run, he was later cornered by police before leaping to his death.

SERIAL KILLERS TRUE CRIME

Chapter 7
SCOTT WILLIAM COX

Born: November 3, 1963

Died: N/A

AKA: Thomas Wood, Thomas Perkins

Active in: Portland Oregon

Sentenced to: 25 years in prison and a lifetime of supervision

As far as convicted serial killers go, Scott William Cox doesn't rate. He admitted to killing a pair of women in the early 90s and served 20 years in prison for his crimes. What makes Cox worthy of this list, however, is the fact that he is on lists across the nation as a possible suspect in more than 20 unsolved murder cases. In one of these cases, he is the only suspect and was known to be in the area at the time the murder occured. That case remains the only cold case in the history of Mountlake Terrace County. He is also considered one of the likely suspects to be the Green River Killer, though he might not be old enough depending on the theory you subscribe to.

He currently lives in Yamhill County in Oregon where he has already been arrested 6 times for violating his parole since 2013. This began in July of 2013, shortly after he was released when he asked for permission to go to the beach and his GPS monitoring unit showed he took an odd, unapproved route. The very next month he visited the home of a woman he was seeing despite not being legally allowed to be around her children.

Early life

Starting when he was 12 years old, Cox was admitted to mental institutions more than 100 times before he was arrested for murder. He also had a history of gun and forgery charges as well. In fact, when he was arrested for murder, he was living quite comfortably under post-prison supervision after being arrested for forgery. Prior to being convicted he worked as a truck driver, often traveling as far as Mexico or Canada and often all the way across the country to places like Ohio. His track record of violence against women, his history of murder and the long distances he traveled have made him a primary suspect in other murders that have occurred along this route during times when he could have conceivably been in the area.

Murders

In November of 1990, a woman named Rheena Ann Bruson, was found in front of a grocery store in Portland, Oregon. She had cuts all over her body, was severely beaten and had been handcuffed. She had also been stabbed through the heart and left for dead. She was found alive but died before she could receive proper medical care.

A few months later in February, a woman named Victoria Rhone was found in a local railyard. She was bound with a man's shirt and then strangled to death. These murders went unsolved for several years.

On May 30, 1991, another female victim was found in downtown Seattle. She had been raped, bitten, beaten and left for dead. She also had marks on her neck that showed she had been strangled and a wine bottle had been forced into her rectum. The woman survived, but never pressed charges and ultimately moved out of the state. Despite the victim's unresponsiveness, police believed that this was the work of the same person who had perpetrated the other killings. They found a witness who had seen the woman be thrown from the truck and were able to find out that it belonged to a company named Woodland Trucking.

Once the company was contacted, they had a name, Seth Scott Cutter. Cutter claimed he was just trying to help the woman and, as the DNA evidence from the scene was not yet available, they had to let him go. Additional research revealed that Cutter had also assaulted another woman in late 1990. Fearing that he was the serial killer, police issued an alert, which police in Newberg Oregon realized was for Scott William Cox, Cutter's real name.

Conviction

Cox was arrested and charged with creating false identification along with additional charges of gun theft in Medford of the same year. He served 6 months in a county jail. While he was in jail, detectives opened up a murder investigation into him for the murder of Rheena Ann Brunson for which he ultimately confessed. He claimed he was mad at his girlfriend and wanted to blow off some steam by beating up a prostitute, things went too far, he stabbed her in the heart and left her for dead. He also confessed to killing Victoria Rhone and beating other women but to no additional murders.

In September of 1993 he plead no contest to two counts of murder for which he was sentenced to a pair of consecutive 150-month sentences. The district attorney at the time explained that the case was hurt by the way in which police investigators obtained evidence which caused a number of key confessions to be dismissed in court. The year after Cox was convicted the state passed new laws regarding capital punishment. If the law had been passed earlier Cox would be serving a 50-year sentence for his crimes.

Chapter 8
KEITH HUNTER JESPERSON

Born: April 6, 1955

Died: N/A

AKA: The Happy Face Killer

Active in: Wyoming, Washington, Oregon, Nebraska, Florida, California

Sentenced to: Life imprisonment without the possibility of parole

Keith Hunter Jesperson killed at least 8 women during the early 90s and earned the moniker the Happy Face Killer from the smiley faces that he always included on his letters to the authorities as well as to the media. He typically targeted prostitutes as well as transients with no apparent rhyme or reason for the killings. He primarily killed his victims via strangulation, in much the same way he killed animals as a child. There was a movie made about his killing spree *Happy Face Killer* which premiered in 2014.

Early life

Born in 1955, Jesperson was the middle child amongst a pair of brothers and a pair of sisters. His father was both an alcoholic, as well as abusive and Jesperson's childhood was violent and troubled. He grew to a large size at a young age but was teased for his size by both his family and his peers. It was during this period that he was found to be torturing and killing animals. Twice before he graduated high school he attempted to kill other children who crossed him, though no serious legal ramifications came from his actions. However, there were ramifications at home, as there were every time Jesperson misbehaved. His father would often beat him with a belt and on at least one occasion administered a strong electric shock.

In addition to torturing and killing animals himself, he has admitted to also forcing them to fight each other and the feeling he got when he forced them to kill. This progressed as he aged until he was trapping and beating to death dogs, cats and birds in the trailer park where he lived, something he claims his father approved of. In the years between this point and when he started killing he has since said that he often reminisced about those times and what it would be like to do such things to a human.

Despite his troubled childhood, Jesperson successfully graduated high school and found work as a truck driver before marrying Rose Huckle and having three children. Things seemed to be going alright for Jesperson for a time but 15 years later he was divorced and his long-time dream, to become a Royal Canadian Mounted Policeman was suddenly shattered by a serious foot injury. When he was able to work again he went back to truck driving, and soon later he began to kill.

Murders

Jespersen's first victim was Taunja Bennett in January of 1990 and took place near Portland Oregon. He met Bennett at a bar and brought her back to a house he was renting in hopes of having sex with her. When Bennett refused, Jespersen struck her. He then proceeded to keep hitting her until she died. He immediately changed his clothes and then went back out drinking in order to ensure he had an alibi. Later that evening he returned home to dispose of the body. The next day he was on the road again and the police were left with no leads and no suspects.

Jespersen was hoping that the killing would gain media attention so he confessed to it by writing a confession on the wall of a local truck stop. This confession didn't garner any attention as the media and the police were looking in another direction so Jespersen decided to take things up a notch. He sent a six page letter to the local paper where he revealed the details of the killing along with a smiley face.

Jespersen's next kill didn't occur until August of 1992. He raped and killed a woman in Blyth California, though he can't remember her name, claiming it is either Cindy or Carla. Jespersen started relishing in the kill at this point and his next victim appeared less than a month later in Turlock California, a prostitute named Cynthia Lyn Rose. Two months later another body, that of Laurie Ann Pentland, a prostitute from Salem Oregon, was found. Jespersen claims she tried to overcharge him for sex based on the fee they had already agreed on, then threatened to call the police so he strangled her.

Jespersen then experienced a bit a lull, lying low for the next 6 months until June of 1993 when he killed an unknown homeless person in Santa

Nella California. The next murder didn't occur until 1994 when another homeless person named Susanne was found beaten to death in Crestview, Florida.

Early in 1995, a woman named Angela Surbrize arranged to have Jesperson give her a ride from Washington to Indiana as he was already headed in that direction. Roughly a week into their trip, Surbrize started to nag Jesperson about how long the trip was taking and how she wanted to get to Indiana. Jesperson took her outburst as an excuse to rape and murder her before strapping her body to the underside of his truck and dragging it face down to remove any identifying characteristics from the body. The remains were only found once Jesperson told the police to look.

In March of that same year, Jespersen decided that his long-term girlfriend, Julie Ann Winningham, was only interested in him for his money so he murdered her as well. This was the only known victim that had any direct connection to him which is what put the police on his trail.

Capture

Jespersen was arrested on March 30, 1995 for the murder of his former girlfriend. He had been questioned the previous week but released due to lack of evidence, and was certain he was going to be caught. Ultimately, he turned himself in after a pair of failed suicide attempts in hopes that the courts would grant him some leniency. Before doing so he wrote his brother a letter claiming to have killed eight people which caused agencies across the country to reopen old cases.

Chapter 9
ORVILLE LYNN MAJORS

Born: April 24, 1961

Died: September 24, 2017 (heart attack)

AKA: Angel of Death

Active in: Indiana

Sentenced to: 360 years in prison

Orville Lynn Majors was a licensed practical nurse who was convicted of murdering patients at Vermillion County Hospital, the hospital he worked at, who added to his workload or were whiny or demanding. He was tried for a total of 6 murders but is suspected of as many as 130 which would have occurred between 1993 and 1995.

Suspicion naturally started to rise at the hospital as, prior to his time there, the average number of deaths per year was low, at less than 30. Meanwhile, during his tenure the rate jumped so dramatically that nearly 1 in every 3 patients who were admitted to the hospital ended up dying. What's more, a patient was more than 43 times as likely to die when he was on duty than when he was not. This equated to roughly a death a day while he was working as opposed to a death every 3 weeks otherwise.

The state of Indiana soon launched an investigation against him and he was arrested in December of 1997. At his trial, a total of 79 witnesses testified against him, several of whom testified that he hated the elderly and had repeatedly been heard saying they should all be gassed.

The investigation lasted a total of 33 months and looked into a total of 165 deaths that occurred at the hospital while Majors was employed there. All told, more than 15 bodies were exhumed and the investigation required more than 90,000-man hours. Ethel Rozsa, Margaret Hornick, Mary Ann Alderson, Cecil Ivan Smith, Luella A. Hopkins, and Freddie Dale Wilson, who were between the ages of 55 and 90, came into the hospital in stable condition and then died while under Major's care.

The prosecutor in the case claimed that Majors liked the feeling of playing God and often injected potassium chloride into IVs which is known to kill at high concentrations. Of the initial 7 unexpected deaths it was proven that Majors was the only person present at 6 of the 7 which explains his eventual conviction.

One particularly damming witness was Paula Holdaway who testified that she saw Majors give her mother, Dorothea Hixon an injection, kiss her forehead and tell her that everything was going to be all right now. No more than a minute later Hixon died. All told, statistical studies linked him to as many as 130 out of the 147 deaths that occurred in the ICU, mostly due to respiratory failure, that occurred between May of 1993 and March of 1995. At one point, every patient in the entire unit died while he was on duty.

The news came as a shock to residents of the small community in Indiana where the hospital was located. Many people knew Majors personally and generally everyone thought of him as a compassionate man with a sense of humor. So compassionate in fact that he was said to have once performed mouth to mouth on a fish that jumped out of an aquarium at a pet store he owned once he was fired from the hospital.

During the trial Majors steadfastly maintained his innocence claiming that he could never kill anyone, would never play God. He even confronted the accusing family members on national television, once on Phil Donahue's show and then again on Montel Williams' show. Nevertheless, a search of his home would eventually reveal both epinephrine and potassium chloride, two drugs that could have caused other mysterious deaths at the hospital. Following the case, the hospital changed its name from Vermillion County Hospital to West Central Community Hospital.

Majors never officially admitted his guilt while he was alive and all that is available when it comes to understanding his motives are the documents from the court case, the most likely of which was drugs. In July of 1994, an affidavit from one of his coworkers notes a distinct change in Majors' personality. The previously personable coworker had now been seen openly injecting methamphetamines. This accusation was confirmed by Tony Towell, owner of a heating and cooling company who confirmed that Majors offered to sell him a stimulant that could be mixed with methamphetamine when he was installing a furnace for him.

Majors' mood continued to deteriorate and coworkers noticed it was hard to get him to do anything he didn't want to do. People who knew him remember during this period of time that he referred to the families of patients as either dirt, white trash or whinners. An employee who once did a safety inspection of the ICU recalled that Majors, who was the only one in the ICU at the time, claimed that he said he was waiting for the old woman to die when asked what he was doing there.

Once incarcerated, Majors turned down numerous media requests for interviews. He held numerous jobs in prison, including as a janitor and by all accounts appeared to be a model prisoner, receiving just 3 minor infractions in all the time he spent there.

Chapter 10
CLEOPHUS PRINCE JR.

Born: July 25, 1967

Died: N/A

AKA: The Clairemont Killer

Active in: California

Sentenced to: Death

Cleophus Prince Jr., known to the media as the Clairemont Killer is responsible for the murder and rape of six women in San Diego County between January of 1990 and September of 1990. In each instance he would enter the residence of his victims during daylight hours and surprise them just after they were through bathing before stabbing them with a kitchen knife. Prince nearly escaped capture multiple times as he was lucky enough to commit his crimes in areas where other more probable suspects lived. The most unique thing about Prince's case is that, as a black man, his victims were all white. In general serial killers are known to primarily target victims of their own race.

Early life

Prince was born shortly after his parents, Celophus Sr. and Dorothy were married and was raised in Birmingham, Alabama. Prince and his family have been tight-lipped about his early life, though it is known that his father spent most of the early part of his life serving 11 years of a 40-year murder sentence and that one of his uncles killed their wife with an automatic rifle. At one point his father was also accused of raping a young woman while his mother held her down. However, on the topic of race, his family claims that the subject was never especially heated in their household and that

Price was taught that prejudice of any type was wrong.

Prince didn't graduate from high school, though he wasn't an especially unruly youth, but did join the Navy when he was 20 in order to get out of Alabama. He was trained at the Great Lakes Naval facility outside of Chicago before being assigned to a Naval Air Station in San Diego and working as a mechanic.

He was court marshaled in October of 1989 and was sentenced to a month in the brig for larceny, shortly before being discharged two months later. It was at this point that he moved into the Buena Vista Gardens apartments, soon to become his hunting grounds and the scene of several of his murders.

Murders

Prince's first victim was Tiffany Paige Schultz in January 1990 in an apartment complex near

Prince's home. Schultz's boyfriend was initially arrested for the crime but was later released. The second murder was Janene Marie Weinhold who was killed in February and Prince's DNA was found at the scene.

Holly Suzanne Tarr was killed in early April while staying with her brother in the same apartment complex. Tarr's death was enough to convince police that there was a serial killer who was stabbing women in the area. Prince kept a ring that previously belonged to Tarr to give to his girlfriend that December.

Elisssa Naomi Keller was murdered in May of 1990, shortly after Prince moved into the East San Diego apartment complex. While no one suspected him at the the time, a gold nugget that was known to be in Naomi's possession was later traced back to Keller from the pawn shop where he sold it.

Pamela Clark was murdered September 13, 1990 in University City. Again, Prince wasn't suspected at the time but later his roommates testified that he was eventually in possession of Clark's wedding ring. Along with Pamela, Prince also murdered Amber Clark, her daughter. By the time the Clarks had been discovered, it was not clear to the police that they were dealing with a serial killer but nevertheless the team assembled to catch the Clark's murders was considered the largest in the history of San Diego.

Unfortunately, they still didn't have much to go on besides the largely useless picture and the fact that the killer always followed the same predictable pattern. It was not discovered until later that the link to many of the women was the Miramar health club where Prince would find them, follow them home, wait to see if they appeared likely to take a shower once they got home and then plot his entrance while they cleaned up so he could be waiting as they came out of the shower.

Capture

While Prince was careful with each of his murders, eventually by April of 1990 a composite description and drawing of him emerged, based in large part on the eyewitness account of a janitor who saw him leaving the complex around the time the police assumed Holly Tarr's death occurred. Unfortunately, the drawing wasn't terribly detailed and it lead the police to focus on a known rapist who lived in the area until January of 1991.

The primary reason for the abrupt change in direction came about due to the fact that Prince botched his next murder in February 1991. He attempted to break into a home near the Miramar health club where he had initially stalked several of his other victims. She was preparing to get into the shower when she heard a noise at the front door. Rather than checking to see what it was, which would have likely cost her, her life, she ran next door and found a neighbor who then confronted Prince directly.

Corner, Prince muttered out an excuse that he was trying to find the home of a female friend and hurried away. Unconvinced, the woman took down his license plate number and called the police. She was then able to match him to the earlier drawing and he was taken into custody without incident on February 4, 1991 in the parking lot of the Miramar health club. Once arrested, Prince consented to provide both saliva and blood samples and the resulting DNA test proved that he had murdered Janene Weinhold. The other murders were then connected to him based on their similar patterns.

After providing the requested samples, Prince was released as the police did not yet have anything to charge him with. He then immediately left California and went to visit his family in Birmingham, Alabama. Once there, he also immediately is arrested for a minor theft charge. On March 2 he is released on bail and the next day the local authorities get the call that the results are back on the murder charge. To ensure Prince doesn't try anything, they call him down claiming he needed to fill out some additional paperwork. Once in the station he was arrested and extradited back to California.

Prince was quickly ordered to stand trial and, despite the fact that his lawyer tried to get half of the charges thrown out based on a lack of evidence, was eventually found guilty in July of 1993 of 6 counts of first degree murder along with 21 other felony charges. After much jury deliberation the jury rendered a verdict of death and the judge agreed to the death sentence in November of that year. Prince's appeal was denied by the Supreme Court in 2007.

Chapter 11
DAVID PARKER RAY

Born: November 6, 1939
Died: May 28, 2002 (heart attack)
AKA: Toy-Box Killer
Active in: New Mexico, Arizona
Sentenced to: Life in prison

David Parker Ray, more commonly known as the Toy-Box Killer, is believed to have kidnapped, tortured and murdered more than 60 people near the New Mexico, Arizona border over several decades. Ray would keep his victims in a trailer known as his toy-box which was exceedingly well equipped for all manner of sexual torture and murder. He was convicted of torture and kidnapping in 2001 but never confessed to the full extent of his crimes.

Early life

As a child Ray lived with his grandfather, though he regularly saw his father who used the opportunity to abuse him physically and mentally. Ray was an exceedingly shy child, especially around the opposite sex, which lead to a great deal of bullying from his peers.

He started drinking heavily and using drugs as a teenager and it is around this time that is believed that his fantasies regarding the murder, rape and torture of women developed. When he was 16 his sister discovered a notbook full of drawings vividly detailing these acts though nothing serious came of the discovery. Ray completed high school without any real incident before working as an auto mechanic and eventually joining the army and eventually being honorably discharged.

Murders

It is unknown exactly when Ray decided to soundproof a trailer that he could tow with his truck for the purpose of (at the very least) raping and torturing his victims. What is known is that when the trailer was found it contained saws, surgical blades, leg-spreading bars, clamps, straps, pulleys, chains and whips to name a few. The room also included a wide variety of sex toys, additional implements of torture, syringes for unknown purposes and a wide variety of diagrams outlining various ways to inflict pain. There was also a homemade generator so he could administer electric shocks.

In the center of the room was a gynecological table modified with a wide range of straps. Ray then further restrained his victims using numerous wooden contraptions that immobilized them in other ways and for other uses, including holding them still while his dogs used them sexually. There was a mirror mounted in the ceiling so the victims could see everything that was being done to them. He also recorded the audio of everything that happened in the room so that his victims would hear it whenever they were conscious.

Capture

Ray was able to escape capture by preying on the transient nature of traffic near the Arizona and New Mexico border. In March of 1999 he approached Cynthia Vigil, a prostitute, at a local truck stop. He claimed to be an undercover police officer and told her that he was arresting her for prostitution. He handcuffed her and put her in his trailer before taking her back to his home in Elephant Butte, New Mexico.

He raped and tortured her for 3 days but she didn't let him break her will to live. She planned her escape and never lost her head, managing to secure the keys to trailer when Ray's current accomplice, Cindy Hendy, left them on a table while she went into another room to use the phone. With the keys Vigil was able to unlock her restraints but before she could escape, Hendy returned to the room and a fight ensued. During the fight Hendy nearly got the upper hand when she broke a lamp over Vigil's head but Vigil rallied and managed to stab Hendy in the neck using a nearby icepick.

Hendy fell to the floor and, not waiting to see if she survived, Vigil fled from the trailer naked, save for a slave collar and some padlocked chains. After escaping, Vigil fled to a nearby neighbor's house who then called the police. Her escape directly leads to the capture of Ray and Hendy in short order. Once Ray was arrested the publicity surrounding the case leads another woman, Angelica Montano to come forward. She told a similar story to Vigils and claimed to have gone to the police who never followed up on her claims.

When he was arrested, Ray was also found to be in possession of a tape from 1996 showing another victim, Kelli Garret. Garret was later identified living in Colorado and told police that she had been kidnapped after Ray's daughter drugged her beer and Ray hit her over the back of the head after she still managed to make it outside.

Once she was unconscious she was taken to the trailer and shackled with a heavy leash and dog collar. She remembers bits and pieces of the next 2 days amidst the torture and date rape drugs. On the third day Ray slashed her throat and, thinking he had killed her, dumped her body on the side of the road near Caballo New Mexico. When she reported what had happened, no one believed her. Her husband assumed she had been cheating on him and had been attacked for her troubles. She later filed for divorce and moved out of the state.

The investigation revealed a total of 2 additional accomplices including Ray's daughter Glenda Jean Ray and Ray's friend Dennis Yancy. Yancy later admitted to killing a woman that Ray had previously kidnapped and tortured and was later convicted to 30 years in prison. After his imprisonment, Ray also allegedly confessed to murdering another accomplice Billy Bowers, though this was never confirmed.

After the arrest the FBI sent more than 100 field agents to scour Ray's property but found no human remains. However, Ray mentioned in his tapes that he drugged women with phenobarbital and sodium pentothal which are both known to cause amnesia so there is no telling how many victims of one sort or another that are out there. One woman assumed her assault had just been a bad dream until she was contacted by the FBI.

Chapter 12
JOHN EDWARD ROBINSON

Born: December 27, 1943

Died: N/A

AKA: Internet's First Serial Killer

Active in: Kansas, Missouri, online

Sentenced to: Death

John Edward Robinson was convicted in 2003 of 3 murders before admitting to 5 more and authorities believe it likely that there are other unknown victims as well. As he found most of his victims in the 90s using the internet, he is often called the internet's first serial killer.

Early life

Robinson was born in Illinois the third of 5 children born to a strict mother and an alcoholic father. Despite this less than ideal upbringing, he went on to be an Eagle Scout and even traveled to England to perform for the Queen. When he was 14 he was admitted to Quigley Preparatory Seminary in Chicago but left after just one year.

When he was 18 he enrolled in Morton Junior College in order to become an X-ray technician but dropped out from there as well after just 2 years. From there he moved to Kansas City and married Nancy Jo Lynch who gave birth to their first child soon after. By 1971 they had a son, a daughter and a mixed pair of twins and were settling in to suburban life.

Robinson was arrested for the first time in 1969 in Kansas City for embezzling more than $30,000 from a local medical practice where he was working as an X-ray technician thanks to some forged documents. He was given 3 years of probation for his crimes. The next year he violated his probation and moved back to Illinois without informing his probation officer to take a job as an insurance agent.

In 1971 he was arrested from embezzling from his new employer and ordered to return to Kansas City for extended probation. In 1975 he was arrested again for mail as well as securities fraud for a fake medical consulting company he was running in Kansas City.

Throughout this time, Robinson outwardly appeared every bit the concerned community member and loving family man. He was a Sunday school teacher, baseball coach, scoutmaster and even on the board of directors for a local charity group. He also had a wide variety of forged letters from the mayor and other civic leaders discussing the great things he had supposedly done for the community. He even got the organization to name him its man of the year.

In 1980 he was again arrested for check forgery and embezzlement which earned him 60 days in jail. Around this time, he claimed to have joined a secret sadomasochist cult known as the Council of Masters and further claimed that he was now a slave maser who was in charge of luring unsuspecting victims to cult torture orgies.

Murders

In 1984, after starting yet another pair of fraudulent companies, Robinson hired a woman named Paula Godfrey to work in sales. She told her family that she was being sent away from training and was never heard from again. Her parents eventually filed a police report and they questioned Robinson who denied having any knowledge of her whereabouts. Several days after the questioning, the Godrey's received a letter from their daughter saying she was fine and did not wish to see them so the investigation was terminated. Paula Godfrey was never seen nor heard from again.

Using the name John Osborne, Robinson met Lisa Stasi in 1985. She and her newborn daughter were staying at a women's shelter near Kansas City and Robinson promised her a job and a place to stay in Chicago along with free childcare for her baby. He is also known to have asked her to sign several blank sheets of paper that were ostensibly to be used to fill in contract details with later. Less than a week later, Robinson got in touch with a couple he knew that was having trouble adopting via traditional channels saying that he had found them a child from a woman that had committed suicide. He collected $5,500 for his trouble and supplied the unsuspecting couple with Stasi's child and the relevant forged documents so they would assume everything was on the level. Stasi was never seen or heard from again.

In 1987, Catherine Clampitt arrived in Kansas City in order to find work. She was hired by Robinson who promised her a traveling sales job in addition to a complete new wardrobe. He was the last person seen speaking to her after she disappeared in June 1987 and her missing person's case was never closed.

Between 1987 and 1993 Robinson was behind bars for more fraud convictions. When he was released he took the prison librarian with him back to Kansas City to work for him. Her name was Beverly Bonner and, soon after she arranged for her alimony checks to be forwarded to a post office in Kansas, she was never heard from her again. Her checks were forwarded to the post office for several years and Robinson continued cashing them as long as they arrived.

By 1993 Robinson had discovered the internet and often frequented chatrooms looking for submissive sexual partners. One early victim was Shelia Faith who met Robinson, moved to Kansas City with her daughter, forwarded her pension checks and then disappeared. Robinson continued cashing her checks for 7 years. In 1999 he signed a legally binding slave agreement with Izabela Lewicka which gave him control over every aspect of her life, including her bank accounts, she disappeared that summer.

Finally, in late 1999 a woman named Suzette Touten moved to Kansas to allegedly travel the world as his sex slave. Her mother received signed letters from her daughter that were supposedly sent from abroad though they all bore Kansas postmarks. The letters were also much more composed than anything her daughter had previously written. When he met Suzette's mother sometime later he told her that her daughter had run off after stealing money from him.

Capture

Years of literally getting away with murder had left Robinson sloppy and careless and by 1999 he had already attracted the attention of authorities both in Missouri and Kansas as him name continued to be associated with missing person investigations. He was ultimately arrested in June of 2000 on a farm he owned outside of La Cygne, Kansas after one woman charged him with stealing her sex toys and another accused him of sexual battery.

The accusation of theft finally gave them the probable cause needed to search his property. When they did so they found the bodies of both Suzette Trouten and Izabela Lewicka in a pair of large chemical drums. At the same time authorities were searching his storage facility in Missouri where he had a pair of large rental spaces. Inside they found 3 more chemical drums containing bodies that were eventually identified as Sheila Faith, her daughter Debbie Faith and Beverly Bonner. All of the women were determined to have been killed by a blow to the head with a blunt instrument.

Robinson stood trail in 2002 in the longest criminal trial in Kansas history. He was convicted for the murders of Lisa Stasi, Isabella Lewicka and Suzette Trouten and received the death sentence.

Chapter 13
JOSEPH MICHAEL SWANGO

Born: October 21, 1954

Died: N/A

AKA: Dr. Death

Active in: New York, South Dakota, Ohio, Illinois

Sentenced to: three life terms without parole

Joseph Michael Swango was a licensed doctor who earned the moniker Dr. Death from his penchant for poisoning. He is suspected of being the cause of as many as 60 deaths though he has only admitted to 4 so far. He was captured in the late 90s and sentenced in 2000 to 3 consecutive life sentences.

Early life

Swango was the middle child of Muriel and John Swango who was an officer in the army and served in Vietnam. When he returned from Vietnam, he developed a drinking problem as well as depression and divorced Swango's mother. Swango was the valedictorian of his high school when he graduated in 1972 and also played the clarinet in the band.

After high school he joined the Marines where he served until he received an honorable discharge in 1976. He never saw active duty but his time in the Marines left him with a commitment to physical fitness and when he wasn't studying for medical school he was typically seen working out around the campus of Quincy University. He ultimately graduated summa cum laude and was awarded the

American Chemical Society Award that same year. He then attended medical school at Southern Illinois University School of Medicine.

It was at this time that Swango's behavior took a turn for the unsettling. When he was undeniably an excellent student in the classroom, he much preferred working as an ambulance driver as opposed to focusing on his studies. This was because he appeared to be fascinated with dying patients, something that was noted at the time though no one thought much of it. After this point, some of Swango's patients ended up dying or almost dying with at least 5 not surviving a ride with Swango when by all accounts they should have.

Swango's medical school performance was not nearly as exceptional as his undergraduate work and he managed to make it out of medical school with a poor evaluation from the school's dean. Nevertheless, he managed to obtain a surgical internship at Ohio State University's medical center in 1983, followed by a residency in neurosurgery.

While he was working in OHU, nurses started complaining that otherwise healthy patients would start dying mysteriously and with dramatic frequency. Each time this occurred it was noted that Swango was the resident on the floor at the time. He was even seen at one point injecting "medicine" into an IV bag. The nurse's concerns were met with an arbitrary review that cleared him of any wrong doing in 1984. Nevertheless, his work was poor so the hospital discontinued his residency that June.

In July 1984, Swango began working for the Adams County Ambulance Corps, despite already being fired from another ambulance company for making a heart attack patient drive himself to the hospital. Soon after he started working for the company, many of the employees started noticing that if Swango made the coffee or brought in the donuts then many of then became sick, often violently and for days on end.

In October of that year, his coworkers brought some of their concerns to the police, Swango's home was searched and several poisons, arsenic among them, were found on the premises. Swango was then sentenced to 5 years in prison for poisoning his coworkers.

In 1989 Swango was released from prison and began working as a lab technician at ATICoal in Newport Virginia. While he was working there many of the other employees sought medical treatment for increasingly serious stomach pains.

In 1991 he changed his name to Daniel J. Adams in order to apply for a residency program in West Virginia. Instead, he was able to get a job at the Sanford Medical Center in South Dakota. He did so via forged documents that restored his physician credentials and general good standing in the community. He also forged a restoration of civil rights letter to allow him to resume practicing medicine despite having a criminal record, though not for poisoning.

Swango soon made a positive name for himself at Sanford, but grew cocky and tried to join the AMA with his new name. The American Medical Association was more thorough which cost him his job. During this time, he had met and married Kristen Kinney, who soon began to develop increasingly painful headaches. When she ultimately left Swango the headaches stopped.

Unfortunately the AMA ultimately lost track of Swango and he found work at the Stony Brook School of Medicine in New York which treated veterans. Almost immediately his patients began dying once again in higher than average numbers. Around this time, his ex-wife was said to have committed suicide, though a high level of arsenic was found in her system.

Swango was once again found out and ousted from the school, though this time he wasn't so lucky. Due to the fact that the school dealt with veterans, the FBI took an interest in the situation.

Capture

With the heat on his activities at an all-time high, Swango laid low until the end of 1994 when the FBI found him living in Atlanta and working as a chemist. Swango was soon fired and the FBI obtained a warrant for using fake credentials to obtain his last job at the veteran's hospital.

Before they could catch him, however, Swango fled to Zimbabwe where he found work as a doctor using additional forged documents. His patients began dying mysteriously, however, and the director became suspicious and fired him. He then rented a room from a woman who soon became violently ill. Her friends consulted a local surgeon who ran a toxicology screen on her that came back positive for arsenic. These results ultimately made their way back to the FBI who soon tracked Swango down in Zimbabwe.

They were too late, however, and Swango remained on the run, finding work for a time in Zambia and ultimately Saudi Arabia. He was charged in abstentia with the poisonings and ultimately caught during a layover flight on his way to Saudi Arabia in the Chicago O'Hare International airport. He was ultimately sentenced to 3 life sentences for his crimes.

Conclusion

Thank you for making it through to the end of *Serial Killers True Crime:13 Serial Killer Murder Stories of the 90s*, and hopefully it hasn't scared you too badly. What you see here is only a slice of the serial killers that were abroad during the 1990s but they are certainly some of the ones that managed to leave the largest legacies of terror behind them.

If you were looking for patterns here, then you were likely disappointed. while all of the individuals were men, and many were from broken homes, aside from that the similarities are few and far between. They came from loving homes and hateful ones, spent their lives destitute or well off, had a problem with authority or served honorably in the Marines. Likewise, for every loaner there was someone who was genuinely liked in the community and for every sexual fetish there is someone who just wanted to make sure they were going to get off work on time. All told, it is hard to spot a serial killer with anything other than hindsight, which is what makes them so fascinating to study and so terrifying to consider encountering on a dark and lonely night.

Finally, if you found this book enjoyable, a review on Amazon is always appreciated!

CPSIA information can be obtained
at www.ICGtesting.com
Printed in the USA
LVHW082132060720
659924LV00011B/597